SKAGW

MW00736652

GOLD RUSH
CEMETERY

History and Guidebook
by Glenda J. Choate

Alaska Archives Resource
and Records Management

Lynn Canal Publishing
Skagway, Alaska

PHOTO CREDITS

ORIGINAL MAPS BY ROLLAND SCHLICK
UPDATED BY JEFF BRADY

Copyright © 1989, 2000 by Glenda J. Choate,
Alaska Archives Resource and Records Management

REVISED EDITION

ISBN: 0-945284-01-2

PRINTED IN WHITEHORSE, YUKON, CANADA

Direct inquiries to:
Lynn Canal Publishing,
a division of The Skagway News Co.
P.O. Box 1898, 264 Broadway St.
Skagway, Alaska 99840-0498

www.skagwaybooks.com

Introduction

Welcome to Skagway! We wanted you to see all of our town and have a fuller historical experience by visiting our gold rush Cemetery. History is a record of all the things that have happened – and we wanted to show the dark but human side. These brave men and women came from everywhere and represent a variety of cultures and professions. They are your ancestors as well as ours. May we face life with the same courage and sense of adventure as did our Gold Rush ancestors.

We are indebted to the following: Klondike Gold Rush National Historical Park, City of Skagway Museum and Archives, Skagway Public Library, Alaska Historical Library, and Rolland Schlick, civil engineer, who prepared the maps. This publication, now in its second edition, is locally produced in Skagway by two small businesses devoted to recording and preserving the history of Skagway and the Lynn Canal area.

Reading history is an opportunity to expand your vision of the past. The story of Skagway is a rich mythology of characters that continue to live in our imagination, although they sleep on in the Gold Rush Cemetery.

Glenda J. Choate
June 2000

The Grand Adventure

On to the Klondike, circa 1897-1898. this stampeder family is taking their child, dog and possessions up the Chilkoot Trail. Note the young Tlingit boy helping the packer father and family.

Today we still do not fully understand why so many men and women left their homes and families to search for gold in a faraway, unknown land. For most, the adventure was unlike any other in their lives, and we marvel at their courage and daring. Photographic images capture scenes of eager faces lining up to buy passage on northbound ships, selecting the appropriate "Klondyke" equipment and supplies and posing in their gear for pictures to send home to the folks.

Stampeders recorded their experiences in letters home, diaries kept of daily events and through the folklore of telling and retelling their adventures. There was an excitement in being part of the crowd, sharing with comrades the preparation and planning of the journey and giving oneself over to becoming part of the flood of humanity moving north in 1897 and 1898. It was easy to believe that anything which engaged so many people's enthusiasm and interest was right and worth doing. Each came believing there was every chance gold would be found, and he or she would be the lucky

person to claim it.

As people climbed aboard ships in Seattle and San Francisco, they knew this might be their final journey. This trip to the Klondike – wherever it was, and however it could be reached – would be filled with peril. All were vulnerable to the twists and turns of fate, yet promised to use good judgment, take reasonable precautions, make the right choice – and gamble on the gold.

This publication is about the people who didn't make it – those who found no gold, whose luck ran out, their journey ending in Skagway in a cemetery at the edge of town. The gold rush essentially was an experience for the young. They came to Skagway or were just passing through, alone or accompanying others on the grand quest. Fate threw the dice and they lost. In a small way, each person became forever part of the history of Skagway and that most exciting of times, the Klondike Gold Rush. Each contributed to the rich heritage here which is experienced by all who come north today.

The view from Skaguay
Bay in the fall of 1897.
Early stampeders with
their tents and supplies
fill up the beach.

Skaguay, 1897

For thousands of stampeders during the Klondike Gold Rush, Skaguay (as it was spelled until 1899) was a stopping point on the way to the North. Its rapid growth from tents on the beach to an established town of businesses, brothels, dance halls, social organizations, city government, school, and churches took place over months, not years. By October 1897, three months after the first stampeders arrived, Skaguay was a community of 3,000 residents who had thrown up hundreds of tents and 40 wooden buildings. It also had a cemetery north of town that all stampeders passed on their way into the unknown.

Skagway's City Cemetery, as it was known during the gold rush, was actively used from 1897 to 1908. Located 1.5 miles from the downtown business district, it was carved from a tree-covered, rocky hillside. Early photographs show fenced graves, interspersed with tree stumps and boulders, overlooking the Skagway River. Boundaries were fixed by the contours of the hillside.

Today the White Pass and Yukon Route railroad tracks lie between the renamed Gold Rush Cemetery and the river, but in 1897 it was the White Pass Trail and Brackett Wagon Road that separated the cemetery from the river. Stampeders hurried past on their way to the White Pass summit, Lake Bennett, the Yukon River, and the Klondike.

City Cemetery

Fences of wood and metal enclose individual grave sites to separate them from the rocks and debris which cover the cemetery site. Early cemeteries were maintained by private subscriptions and the volunteer donations of labor and materials from local residents. Circa 1899.

The cemetery was a favorite place to visit each year in May on Decoration Day. In May 1899 stores closed, and festivities included a procession to the cemetery and children decorating graves with flowers. In 1900 the Skagway Veterans Club made a Decoration Day cemetery visit to remember old comrades (see next page).

Cemetery maintenance was a volunteer effort by local residents prior to incorporation of the city. On May 13, 1900, the Daily Alaskan reported that D.N. Hugill earlier had started a subscription to put the cemetery in order. He had collected 66 subscriptions amounting to $119 in cash and materials.

The cemetery rapidly filled. By 1908, the Skagway City Council was looking for a new cemetery site which was later found across the Skagway River.

Decoration Day

TO DECORATE

Old Soldiers Will Remember Comrades' Graves.

The old soldiers of Skagway will appropriately observe Decoration Day next Friday. They will march to the cemetery in a body, where the graves of the old soldiers who are reposing there will be decorated with flowers. Capt. Sumerall will detail a squad of soldiers to act as an escort.

All the old soldiers, both resident and visiting Skagway, are requested to meet at the office of Judge I.N. Wilcoxen at 1 o'clock, sharp, Friday afternoon. All those who may wish to donate flowers can either hand them to one of the old soldiers or leave them at Judge Wilcoxen's office.

Rev. M.A. Covington, of the Methodist church, will preach a memorial sermon Sunday to the Grand Army veterans.

So far as known, there are only seven old soldiers now in Skagway. Those are Geo. E. Howard, Judge Wilcoxen, Conductor M.S. Morehouse, Alex. Green, Collector Mintle, B.K. Hall and Thomas Broemser.

The Daily Alaskan, May 1902

TO THE DEAD

Will Devote Day to Nation's Savers.

Throughout the length and breadth of the United States today the people will cease the usual routine of their daily lives and pay their respects to those of that army, whose valor saved the dismemberment of the republic when secession was attempted that have passed from life. While a grateful people all over the United States, north and south, are covering the graves of the heroes of '61 with flowers, those who are at rest in the Skagway cemetery will not be forgotten.

This afternoon the members of the Grand Army of the Republic, a detail of soldiers and the citizens who desire to participate will meet in front of the post office on Fifth avenue at 1 o'clock, sharp. From there they will proceed to the public school building, where the procession will be joined by the school children, and the march to the cemetery will continue. The children are requested to congregate by 1:30 o'clock.

The services at the cemetery will consist of the Grand Army ritualistic burial service. This will be followed by the decoration of the graves of the old soldiers who are interred in the cemetery under Reid's falls.

Decoration Day being a national holiday, the public generally are invited to participate in the services. The busses of the Dewey, Fifth Avenue and Golden North hotels will take any ladies who desire to attend the services as far as the old tollgate. It is not promised that they will remain there until the close of the services if a steamer should arrive.

Rev. M.A. Covington will deliver a memorial sermon Sunday evening. His subject will be, "Our National Perils and Safeguards."

Cemetery Guide

Harry Schofield (No. 13) is mourned by his fellow longshoremen.

1. Martin & Lucy Itjen

As Skagway's first tourism promoter, Martin took a Ford truck chassis and built the unique Skagway Street Car, the town's first tour bus. As part of his promotion of Skagway, Itjen restored Jeff. Smith's Parlor and opened it as a museum. His tour also brought visitors to the Gold Rush Cemetery and Reid Falls. Lucy, his fiancé from Chicago, joined him in Skagway after the Gold Rush.

2. William & Nellie Mulvihill

As chief dispatcher of the White Pass and Yukon Route, William J. Mulvihill had a telegraph line connect the rail depot on Broadway with his home. He worked for the railroad more than forty years and served a record sixteen terms as mayor of Skagway. He and his wife, Nellie, lived for many years in the beautiful home, built by pioneer photographer William Case, which still stands at Seventh and Alaska. Their descendants still live in Skagway. "Mul" is buried near the railroad tracks, so he can hear the trains.

3. Ida Olsen

Ida Olsen had lived most of her life in Skagway prior to her death on June 24, 1908. The death of this 19-year-old woman was particularly poignant. She was the daughter of City Marshal George Dillon. Her granddaughter still lives in Skagway.

4. Annie Moulton Cameron

According to the Daily Alaskan, the death of Mrs. Cameron was a "particularly sad one." She came north via St. Michael in 1897 on the famed Steamer Excelsior, which had carried news of the Klondike gold strike to San Francisco. After wintering in Fort Yukon, she went on to Dawson City, where she operated a hotel and married John Cameron, a member of the North West Mounted Police. After ill health forced her to leave Dawson, she arrived in Skagway in spring 1908 with an arrangement to meet her husband. But he never arrived. She underwent a successful operation for an internal abscess at the Red Cross hospital, but another abscess developed. She was too weak for a second surgery and died on June 21. Attempts were made to find her husband and wire relatives in Battle Creek, Michigan, but no one responded. A short graveside service, conducted by Rev. Good, was attended by ladies who had come to know this friendly pioneer woman during her short stay in Skagway. Ironically, many years later, it was revealed that Mrs. Cameron was a daughter of Clement Thompson, a former mayor of Battle Creek, but she had quit writing her family in 1898. Thanks to Battle Creek resident Frank Thorpe who uncovered this information after a visit to the Gold Rush Cemetery in 1996. To date, however, there has been no new information about why her husband never came to Skagway.

5. Jefferson R. "Soapy" Smith

For nine months in 1897-1898, Jefferson Randolph "Soapy" Smith was Skagway's unofficial and un-elected leader. The Soapy Smith gang eventually managed to offend the more law-abiding citizens of the town, and their leader was shot and killed in a gunfight on the Juneau Co. Wharf on July 8, 1898. Frank Reid was credited with killing Soapy Smith, although a debate rages to this day as to whether he was the vigilante who actually fired the bullet that pierced the desperado's heart. Smith's descendants, who assisted the local Eagles Aerie No. 25 in starting the annual "Soapy's Wake" some years ago, maintain that Soapy was killed by a railroad henchman who was guarding the wharf with Reid, and others say Smith may have been killed accidentally by one of his own men.

We'll never know for sure. Unlike Jesse James, Soapy Smith's body will never be exhumed to determine the truth behind his demise. Soapy's was one of the graves that washed away when Reid Falls Creek flooded on September 12, 1919. See "Bones of Bad Man...." column on the next page.

An early view of Soapy's grave just outside the cemetery's boundary, with the first of many headstones.

BONES OF BAD MAN OF GATEWAY CITY SLUICED IN GREAT CLEANUP

WHITEHORSE - In addition to the great amount of damage it did to the railway track and bridges in the Skagway valley, the recent flood there washed away a time honored attraction that was probably more fit of shivering fear from timid female tourists who viewed it than any other object in Alaska, namely the grave of the famous "Soapy Smith" whose remains were laid to rest in the old cemetery just below Reid Falls not far from the river bank.

Most of the nerve-racking tales of the late lamented Soapy's ferociousness and diablerie that are now in circulation are pure fiction. The writer of this article knew him well, and except when under the influence of liquor, he was as mild a mannered man as ever "scuttled a ship" or "fleeced a sucker." To the gang of sure thing men, grafters and thugs over which he ruled with an iron hand, he was known as a man of reckless courage, quick on the draw and one whom it was not well for a male denizen of the underworld to cross; but to the law abiding and peacefully inclined citizen he was affable, courteous and deferential, and his hand and purse were always open to the cry of distress. In Canada and the U.S. are today men respected and accredited with an honesty they do not possess who are robbing the widows, orphans and disabled soldiers by the manipulation of the price of necessities of life as a means of acquiring the earnings of others; from which that outlaw known as "Soapy Smith" would have turned in abhorrence.

So wage the world. The world can assume the garb of the lamb and no one be the wiser, but for the black sheep to change the color of his fleece is among the impossible.

– *Dawson Daily News* (from Whitehorse Star, Oct. 3, 1919)

The above article was believed to have been written by A.M. Rousseau, then publisher of the Whitehorse Star, who cut his teeth during the Klondike Gold Rush on papers in Skagway with former partner E.J. "Stroller" White. Thanks to Dawson City historian John Gould for passing this news clipping on to us. During subsequent research at the Skagway Public Library, we found that the flood occurred on the evening of September 12, 1919, washing out two railroad bridges and a span of the highway bridge north of town. Three days later a party of men swung from trees across the raging torrent of Reid Falls Gulch and assessed the damage to the cemetery. According to a report in the September 16 Daily Alaskan: "At the head of the cemetery the stream divides into four parts, two going north and two south of the old cemetery. One of the south streams has made its way down through the old cemetery and appears to have cut out the southern line of graves, as well as that of Soapy Smith's. This was evidenced by the number of markers which were lying in different parts."

6. デんザブロー ナカノ
(Densaburo Nakano)

Little is known about Denzaburo Nakano, the cemetery's only Asian occupant, other than he died at Bishop Rowe Hospital from typhoid fever on May 21, 1900. The ornate Japanese burial post was translated for us by Japanese journalist Tumihiro Sakakibara with assistance from local resident Jean Worley, a local Japanese-American who helped him research the death records while she was magistrate, and who wrote Nakano's name in Japanese above.

7. Unknowns

More than one "Unknown" is buried in the cemetery. The most infamous is the man who tried to stage Skagway's only bank robbery at the former Canadian Imperial Bank of Commerce on September 15, 1902. The man tied dynamite to himself and demanded $20,000, at gun point, from a teller. While waiting for his dough, the unknown robber was startled by someone who entered the bank behind him. His gun fired, the dynamite went off, and nothing was left of the man but his head, which no one could identify. The head allegedly was preserved for some time, eventually making its way into Martin Itjen's first museum.

8. Samuel Bridges

The Daily Alaskan reported Samuel Bridges' death of pneumonia at Bishop Rowe Hospital on May 8, 1900. The paper described Bridges as "a laboring man, 48 years old, who came to Skaguay on the last 'City of Seattle' and was taken ill shortly thereafter. Bridges had no friends and the past history of the man's life was not learned."

9. Arthur Hallam

His death was recorded by the Reverend John A. Sinclair in **Mission Klondike**, a book written by Sinclair's son James. Hallam was the grandson of Sir Arthur Henry Hallam, whose death inspired the beautiful poem, "In Memoriam", written by England's poet laureate, Alfred Tennyson. On August 29, 1898, Hallam died from an injury while working on the railroad. His fiancé from Oregon arrived in Skagway just days after his untimely death.

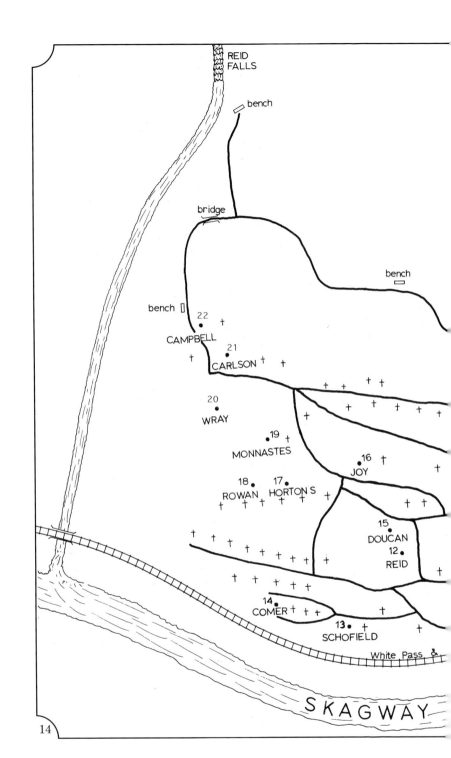

REID
FALLS

bench

bridge

bench

bench

22
CAMPBELL

21
CARLSON † †

20
WRAY

19 †
MONNASTES

16 †
JOY

18   17
ROWAN HORTONS

15
DOUCAN
12
REID

14
COMER † †

13 †
SCHOFIELD

White Pass

S K A G W A Y

14

SKAGWAY, ALASKA'S
GOLD RUSH
CEMETERY

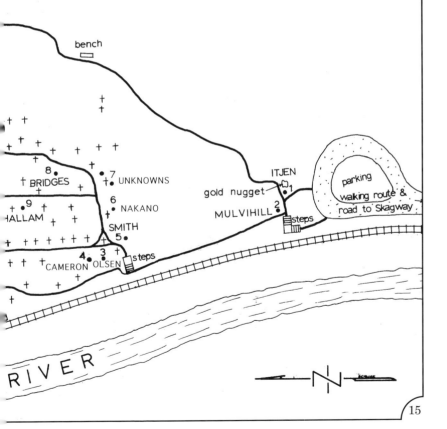

bench

ITJEN

gold nugget

8 BRIDGES

7 UNKNOWNS

6 NAKANO

9

HALLAM

SMITH

5

MULVIHILL

1

2

steps

parking

walking route &

road to Skagway

4 3

CAMERON OLSEN

steps

RIVER

N

10. Hazel Atchison

This little girl was one of the first victims of a cerebral spinal meningitis epidemic in Skagway in the late winter and early spring of 1898. Hazel was born in 1894 and died on February 6, 1898. The Dyea Trail of February 25, 1898 reported: "The mortality in Skaguay is becoming alarming. Seven deaths from spinal meningitis have occurred in the past week and many are sick of the dread disease."

11. Ella Wilson

Little is known of this "Soiled Dove," as the newspapers referred to Skagway's ladies of the evening. Ella was approximately 28 years old when she was strangled to death by "unknown parties" in her house on Holly Street. An interesting note is that although she died on May 28, 1898, an inquest into the cause of her death was not held until after Soapy Smith's death in July.

12. Frank Reid

Until his shoot-out with Soapy Smith, Reid's most important contribution to the growing new town of Skagway was the survey of the new town site. Reid lived for 12 days after being shot by Smith (see pages 28-29). To show their gratitude to Reid and appreciation for his sacrifice, the citizens of the town donated money and erected this monument in his memory. Reid's death on July 20, 1898 marked the end of the lawless chapter of Skagway's history.

13. Harry Schofield

Schofield's death certificate lists both heart failure and alcoholism. A longshoreman, he was found dead in his cabin on November 28, 1903. Schofield's friends erected the impressive grave marker, and the cover photograph vividly captures and documents those gathered and the condition of the cemetery in 1903.

14. Pat Comer

Comer was boating with his friend John Stanley about a mile offshore from the dock at Fort William H. Seward near Haines. It is believed Comer stood up in the boat, fell out, and Stanley, an excellent swimmer, tried to rescue him. But the cold waters of Lynn Canal claimed them both. Soldiers from the dock saw the accident and tried to rescue the victims, but were too late. The accident took place August 2, 1903, and Comer's body was returned to Skagway.

15. Thompson Doucan
20. William Wray

The Skaguay News described Thompson Doucan as a "bughouse barber" who operated the O.K. Barber Shop at the foot of Paradise Alley. While at the O.W. Johnson saloon on the Pacific Coast dock, Doucan shot his former roommate and intimate friend, William Wray. Doucan then turned the gun on himself and committed suicide. The newspaper described Wray as a 36-year-old merchant and boat builder who was inoffensive and well-liked. However, the paper said Doucan possessed a "morose disposition and was considered materially 'off' by those who knew him intimately." Doucan died March 9, 1899, and Wray died later from his wounds.

16. William H. Joy

While on a hunting trip with his son Louis on a mountain near Denver Glacier, Joy accidentally discharged his gun and was injured. The young man left his father and went to get help. The father, regaining consciousness, tried to walk down the mountain but instead fell and was killed in the fall on November 1, 1904.

17. Florence & Bert Horton

A young Skagway grocery store owner and his bride were on their honeymoon camping trip when they were killed near Haines. Their murderers, a group of Indians, buried their bodies and returned to Skagway. Months later, one of the men converted to Christianity at a Salvation Army revival meeting in Skagway and confessed to the crime. His remorse was so great that influential local residents requested leniency at the trial. Six Indians were convicted and sent to McNeil Island in Washington for imprisonment. The Hortons were killed October 24, 1899 and were later re-buried in the Skagway cemetery on March 15, 1900.

18. James Mark Rowan

A deputy marshal in Skagway, young J.M. Rowan was one of the victims of Soapy Smith's reign of lawlessness. In its first issue on February 1, 1898, the Morning Alaskan reported that Deputy U.S. Marshal Rowan was shot and killed the previous evening by bartender John Fay of Smith's gang in People's Theater on Holly Street. Andy McGrath, a local resident, had been short-changed by the bartender and went to get the deputy marshal. When McGrath returned with Rowan, Fay shot the two of them. At the time of the shooting, Rowan's wife was giving birth to their baby. Rowan's death fueled the fires of the vigilantes against Smith, leading to the formation of the Committee of 101. Smith was able to hold them off, temporarily, with his own Citizens Committee of 317, and get Fay shipped out of town to the district jail in Sitka. Five months later, the vigilante committee would lose patience with the gang leader's silver tongue following the daylight robbery of stampeder J.D. Stewart behind Jeff. Smith's Parlor, and Rowan's death would finally be avenged.

19. Walter L. Monnastes

Seventeen-year-old Walter Monnastes was a steward on the steamer "Florence S." on the Thirty Mile River in the Yukon. The boat was racing other boats, but its cargo shifted in a turn, and the vessel capsized. Young Walter and two women passengers died in the accident on July 20, 1900. His body was returned to his family in Skagway for burial.

21. Lillian Theresa Carlson

In its first issue on October 15, 1897, the Skaguay News reported: "Lillian Theresa, daughter of Mr. and Mrs. A.P. Carlson, died Wednesday a.m. October 6, 1897. She was ill but 24 hours. Services are at the family residence. She was born in Everett, Washington on August 19, 1894. The first child to die in Skaguay. She was a bright, beautiful and promising child...."

22. Rev. Archibald J. Campbell

During the winter of 1897-1898, the Union Church in Skagway was shared by five denominations with scheduled services for each. Rev. Campbell was one of Skagway's first clergymen. He studied medicine before becoming a minister and was known in town for his "Magnetized Liver Cure," particularly for the ladies of the town. An elderly man, he died of a heart attack on February 2, 1899.

18

1897-99 Medical Advertisements

N. K. Wilson

DRUGGIST

~Wholesale Medicine~

Outfits for Atlin
and Yukon.

Physician's Prescriptions

Carefully Compounded

Holly Ave, near State.

KOONS & RICHTER, ...
DRUGGISTS, Corner Broadway and Boad,
.... Give us a call.
Drugs, Patent Medicines, Toilet Articles, Etc., Etc..
AT ROUND PRICES.

P. A. E. Boetzkes, M.D.
PHYSICIAN AND SURGEON.

OFFICE : Sixth Ave. between Broadway
and State—Over Peterson's store.

Hours, 9 to 10 a. m.—1 to 2 and 7 to 9 p. m.

Dr. Laycook Barker,
PHYSICIAN AND SURGEON.

Clayson Block.

Office hours: 10 to 12 a. m.
2 to 5 p. m.
7 to 9 p. m.

DENTIST

Dr. Rystron is prepared
to do all kinds of den-
tal work at moderate
prices.

Teeth Extracted Without Pain.

McKinney st., bet. Broadway and
Runnalls.

Funeral Expenses.	$100.00
Ketcham s Cough Syrup.	.15
	$ 99.25

ONE LIFE SAVED.

Sold only by

Kelly & Co,
Druggists.

Stampede Hazards

A majority of the burials in the cemetery occurred in 1898 and 1899. This was a high point in the number of people coming to Skagway and placed a great strain on the town's resources. The railroad was under construction, and families were arriving to join husbands and fathers.

Poor and inadequate sanitation and the 1898 spinal meningitis epidemic contributed to the high death rate. Although Skagway had a number of physicians, dentists, hospitals, and drug stores, death certificates reveal more about health care at the turn of the century than Skagway's inadequacies. Causes listed include congestion of the brain, infantile bowel paralysis, internal abscess, child birth, infant mortality, gunshot, "natural," old age, heart failure, and "unknowns."

Indeed the death statistics are a grim reminder that it was a dangerous and fearful time for all. Inexperienced and inadequately prepared stampeders suffered from the cold and hostile environment, snow slides, and drownings from ice breaking in rivers and lakes. Some simply got lost as they traveled through unknown terrain. Murder and acts of violence often reflected the greed and competition found along the way. Overwhelmed by the hardships, a few chose suicide. They became the sad statistics, but many others lived to tell the stories of their gold rush adventures.

"Have You Seen ...?"

Although every effort was made to document deaths, to return bodies to families or provide a final burial in the cemetery, the local newspapers frequently carried notices and queries from families searching for lost members. Their loved ones said good-bye, went north, and had not been heard from again since Seattle, Dyea, Sheep Camp, Log Cabin, or Bennett. So the inquiries read, "Has anyone seen my son – or my husband – or my brother." For these families, sometimes there was an answer, but often not. The person was simply lost to everyone.

Address of Henry Lubicz. He is a physician and surgeon, but went north four years ago to follow mining. May be known as Dr. Lubicz, Dr. Henry, or "Doc." He is very polite and gentlemanly. There is money and property here awaiting his attention. Address: Ella Shedloski, Kingstown, Indiana.

WHERE IS HE?

Money and Property Waiting Dr. Henry Lubicz.

There is money and property at Kingstown, Indiana, requiring the attention of Dr. Henry Lubicz, a physician and surgeon, who came to Skagway four years ago searching for gold. Ella Shedloski, presumably a relative, is seeking information as to the missing man's whereabouts. The lady writes that he is supposed to be located seven miles from Skagway.

Lubicz is a physician, surgeon and druggist, according to the letter already mentioned, though whether he will be practicing his profession at all is not known. "He has been gone from home just four years and two months," continues the lady. "We have gotten many conflicting reports, some that he was drowned, some murdered, and others that he died of starvation and insanity, but 'the still small voice' has said to me all the time he lives in earth life, and now he has been located seven miles from your town. He might use the name Dr. Henry or Doc.

"He would be known as an all round good man and is very polite and gentlemanly to all. There is property and money he should attend to soon, and we feel as though he must be found this summer, so he can come out before the winter closes."

The Daily Alaskan, May 1902

LOST MEN

Inquiries for Warren Smith and Geo. B. Trimmer.

There seems to be no cessation of the letters being received by the newspapers and postmasters of the North, making inquiry for lost relatives or friends. The last mail brought two inquiries, one to the postmaster and the other a circular letter addressed to editors.

Postmaster Sampson received a letter from Miss Helen Belle Smith, Beatrice, Neb., asking for information as to her father, Warren A. Smith, who, she says, was in and about Skagway for five years and who she thinks must have some friends in the city.

Miss Smith says: "The report has reached me that my father, Warren A. Smith, of your city, died last September in a mining camp. I can hardly believe that if it were so that we would not receive official notice. Of course I am very ignorant of the manner in which you treat such matters or of any of the doings in Alaska. If you cannot give me any information could you send me the address of some one who could."

Warren Smith did carpenter work in Skagway and was at one time employed in the lumber camp getting out logs for the Moore saw mill. He came to Skagway in August 1897 and formerly lived in Port Angeles, Washington. He was frequently called "Michigan" Smith.

The other communication comes from the county police of Rochdale, England, and makes inquiry for George Butterworth-Trimmer. Seaman's discharge papers belonging to the last named were found on the beach at Nome last fall. It is feared that he was drowned on the North coast.

Any information left at the Daily Alaskan office concerning either of these men will be forwarded to the parties interested.

PEOPLE'S FURNITURE FACTORY

An industry which indicates enterprise and a tendency to promote the welfare of Skagway generally, and its promoter in particular, is the People's Furniture Factory and salesrooms, corner of Broadway and Eighth avenue. That indomitable spirit that made Skagway the metropolis of Alaska, permeates E. R. Peoples, as is evidenced by the rapid strides made in the manufacture of many of the articles most in demand here in Skagway and in the interior. His factory and salesrooms are full from garret to basement with furniture of all kinds and descriptions. There is perhaps, no line of business on which there is higher freight charges on the goods handled than on furniture in proportion to the first cost. By manufacturing these goods here in Skagway the freight charges, as well as the jobbers' profit is saved and the customer gets the benefit of low prices for first-class hand-made goods.

Mr. Peoples is a young man of considerable energy and push, and is thoroughly honorable in all his dealings, courteous and obliging, and withal, one with whom it is a pleasure to do business. Parties expecting to locate here or go to the interior will consult their own interests and save money by purchasing their furniture here and not pay freight from the lower country.

Mr. Peoples is also engaged in the undertaking business and keeps on hand a first-class stock of caskets. He has had considerable experience as a funeral director, and is a skilled embalmer. He gives special attention to preparing bodies for shipment. He has the only hearse in Alaska and it is a beauty.

A Needed Service

Early Skagway newspapers carefully chronicled the daily life of the community. Their constant mission, though, was to extol the new town, its virtues and its enterprising residents, so stampeders would be persuaded to take the best way north – through the White Pass.

But tucked in a few lines here and there among the paragraphs of news were the sad reports of the death of a child, a young mother, a victim of violence, or the ravages of disease and sickness among the unfortunate.

By November 1897, Skagway had an undertaker and embalmer, E.R. Peoples, who placed discreet advertisements in the newspapers announcing his presence in the community. A common practice during the Gold Rush was for bodies of the deceased to be returned to their homes "outside of Alaska," and Peoples reminded readers that he specialized in this service.

In December 1899, the Skagway News announced to its readers that there had been no deaths in Skagway in two months, and, because business was so slow, Mr. Peoples would begin to sell furniture and household goods. The furniture business was a more profitable venture for Skagway's first undertaker and embalmer. By 1908, Peoples had moved to Fairbanks and later became mayor of that new Alaskan city.

The Skaguay News - March 1899

23

Sad Death of Mrs. Pauley

Matilda Elizabeth Pauley, the beloved wife of C.A. Pauley, manager of the Pacific Market on Fifth avenue, died of peritonitis on Saturday afternoon, June 11, 1898, in her twenty-fifth year, after a very brief illness. Two weeks previous, on the very day, Mr. and Mrs. Pauley buried their infant daughter, and it appears the lady contracted a severe cold while at the cemetery, which settled on her lungs. The attending physician succeeded in subduing the lung difficulty, but peritonitis set in, and in spite of the best of care and attention, the lady gradually grew weaker until Saturday afternoon, when she quietly passed away in the presence of her sorrowing husband and immediate friends. Mr. and Mrs. Pauley were united in marriage at Pendleton, Oregon in 1892. Their union was a singularly happy one in every way. The deceased lady was a very lovable woman, a dutiful and helpful wife, and very highly respected by all who knew her. Her sudden death, in the prime of young woman and motherhood, was not only a severe blow to the sorrowing husband, but to her friends as well.

The body of mother and child were interred in the Skagway cemetery, for the present, but this fall they will be taken up and removed to the cemetery at Auburn, Wash., their former home. The funeral was held at the Union church, where Dr. Campbell conducted appropriate and impressive ceremonies.

The Skaguay News, June 14, 1898

A Sad Announcement

Mrs. Pauley and her baby were later returned to Oregon. This sad announcement describes the rigors of life in the north for young mothers and their children. In reporting death in the community, newspapers generously informed readers of the virtues and vices of the departed and often were quite judgmental when they felt someone had erred in life. But at the same time, there was an air of solicitude toward the grieving survivors which was an expression of the community's concern and sense of loss.

Skagway Cares

Death in the community often brought out sincere caring and compassion for victims and survivors. More than half of the 500 people in the area who died between 1897 and 1908 were returned to their homes and families in other places. Estates were settled, property returned and families notified whenever possible.

Often Skagway's social organizations – the Elks, Eagles, Masons, and the Arctic Brotherhood – met this need. The Arctic Brotherhood, founded by stampeders on their way north, gave their members final rites and helped to settle financial affairs. Funds were raised from people in the community to build a church, establish a school, a hospital, care for the cemetery, and erect memorials.

The First Hospitals

Skagway's first hospital, established in February 1898, later became Bishop Rowe Hospital.

The first hospital in Skagway opened in February 1898, when the spinal meningitis epidemic ravaged the local community. Money was raised to rent and furnish a hospital building on the corner of McBride Avenue and Ivy Street. On February 23, 1898, the Morning Alaskan reported that "the lot is 50' x 100', house is 1.5 story log, 18' x 24', with a cellar, stable and a large quantity of wood for $600." The paper also reported the following admissions to the hospital that week. Ten patients were cared for with these ailments:

> 1 - frozen toes amputated
> 2 - cerebral spinal meningitis
> 2 - pneumonia
> 2 - grippe
> 1 - bronchitis
> 1 - influenza
> 1 - inflammation of the bowel
> 1 - death

Inside a White Pass & Yukon Route railroad hospital tent. Construction accidents put many workers in the hospital, and others suffered from the effects of weather and the arduous work up the line.

In April the hospital became the Bishop Rowe Hospital, named for Episcopal Bishop Peter Trimble Rowe, its benefactor who made frequent trips to Skagway. Women of Skagway decided the hospital needed a women's ward, and funds were soon raised for the ward. The Bishop Rowe Hospital advertised on April 15, 1899 that "its location was high and healthy, accommodation for 30 patients, clean, well ventilated, with own dispensary with full stock of medicines and three doctors on staff."

During construction of the White Pass and Yukon Route railroad from 1898 to 1900, the company opened hospitals at Camp 7, Log Cabin and Skagway. By September 1900, the Railway Hospital, located at 11th and Broadway (on the site of the present city-operated Dahl Clinic), advertised that it was "thoroughly equipped for every possible medical and surgical emergency."

St. Nicholas Sanitarium, on Main Street between 11th and 12th, was in business in November 1900. The proprietor, Mrs. M.J. Smith, offered boarding and lodging by the day or week.

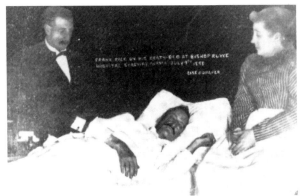

A Hero's Final Days

Frank Reid lived twelve days after being shot on July 8, 1898 with a Winchester .45 by Soapy Smith on the Juneau Co. Wharf. The bullet entered two inches above the groin and fractured the pelvic bone before exiting near his spinal column. Reid was taken to Bishop Rowe Hospital, where a council of the town's leading medical people tried to save his life. But the prognosis was not good, and Reid's final days were long and painful.

Reverend John A. Sinclair, Skagway's Presbyterian minister, was Reid's companion during this time. According to the doctors, Reid's bullet killed Soapy instantly. Sinclair conducted Soapy's last rites at a grave site just outside the cemetery boundary. Only two people were present. Reid read Sinclair' eulogy for Soapy in the newspaper and liked it so much, he almost memorized it. The title of the eulogy was: "The way of the transgressor is hard."

With Sinclair's help, Reid renewed his Christian faith and prepared for the end. To lift the spirits of the lonely man, Sinclair had his church choir visit and sing hymns. There were frequent visits to his bedside. The singing comforted Reid, and music filled his final days.

The town closed down for Reid's funeral. Sinclair conducted part of the service on the street in front of the church, because so many people wanted to attend. At the cemetery, Reid was given a soldier's last rites with prayers by a chaplain, a rifle salute, and the bugle call of "lights out, and rest."

Later, public subscriptions were collected to place a large monument on the grave. During his brief career in Skagway, Frank Reid progressed from bartender, to city engineer, to town hero and burial in the center of the City Cemetery.

Frank Reid Falls

One of the paths out of the Gold Rush Cemetery leads up to a 300-foot cascading stream of water named for Skagway hero Frank Reid, the man who shot and is credited with killing Soapy Smith. The sound of falling water during Reid's funeral so inspired S.R. Ponton that he wrote to the Daily Alaskan to suggest the falls be named for the man who gave his honor for Skagway:

"The tortuous course of the mountain torrent and its final plunge, are typical of the life of the pioneer. The roar of the falls; the wind soughing through the trees, and the brawling of the rapids in the river below, will sound an everlasting requiem over his (Reid's) grave...."

One of the highlights of Martin Itjen's Skagway Street Car Tour was a visit to the Gold Rush Cemetery, Reid Falls and the "World's Largest Nugget." Itjen and his wife were buried near the nugget after they passed away in the 1940s.

Skagway's thank-you to Frank Reid was this impressive monument placed upon his grave some time after his death, and the naming of the falls behind the cemetery. Circa 1899.

Skagway's Journey

By 1905 the stampede to the Klondike was over, and Skagway began its journey through time. The WP&YR railroad moved passengers and freight "over the hill" into the Yukon and Canada. The town had a way to exist and memories to preserve.

Men like Martin Itjen and William John Mulvihill came to Skagway, lived their lives, made their mark, and kept the community moving forward. Itjen made Skagway a town that everyone "had" to visit, because its Klondike Gold Rush past was an intimate part of everyday life. Mulvihill kept the trains moving and the town survived. Skagway and its gold rush history are alive to this day, thanks to these two and others like them.

Today people work, raise families and continue to live in a valley where the train whistle still blows and the past, present and future come together.

Martha L. Schneidewind, who contributed these pictures on a recent visit, was a college sophomore when she first came north on the "SS Prince George" in 1936. Their street car tour, guided by colorful conductor Martin Itjen, was the "highlight of our trip." During a stop at Gold Rush Cemetery, Itjen showed off Soapy guarding the "Worlds' Largest Nugget," which was chained to a nearby tree. Itjen also bragged about his publicized trip to Hollywood to visit Mae West, whom he invited to "come up and see me some time."